Separate Yourself From the Accuser

BY **Ginae Lee Scott**

TURN THE PAGE PUBLISHING

ISBN: 978-0-9837208-9-8

Published by :**Turn the Page Publishing**

www.ginaeleescott.com

Editor: **Margo Dill**

Cover Design: **Jonna Feavel**

To my husband, Scottie, who makes it possible for me to write.

I would also like to thank my friend, Lynn, who walked along with me on the journey of this book, she also allowed me to read the manuscript aloud to her, she is a great listener; and to my daughters, Arielle and Rachel, who constantly imparted wisdom unto me, that is beyond their years, for the heartbeat of this book.

"The accuser of our soul does not come to us in ways so we will recognize him... He does not come in a red suit and holding a pitchfork... No, he comes like the angel of light, beautiful even... once he hooks us in hurt, fear and shame... that is all he has to do."

Be blessed and expect to hear from the unseen spiritual realm of our Lord Jesus Christ as you read from these pages.

What is an Accuser?

What is an accuser? Most people know the meaning of the word, but have we ever given it a lot of thought? We need to know the true meaning of what and who the accuser is; and by attaining that knowledge; it will help us in recognizing the accuser. The true accuser is lurking around us on a daily basis. He is sly, but he is always there. The accuser could be walking around in our life right now, at this very moment, and most of us may not even notice anything is off-balance. Without knowledge, we could be walking in total ignorance. Knowledge is good; and we should seek to learn, so we are not caught off unawares.

An intelligent heart acquires knowledge, and the ear of the wise seeks knowledge.
~ Proverbs 18:15

Satan is the accuser of the brethren. He accuses us day and night before our God; painting a destructive image with wasteful and idle words is the accuser's full-time job. He attacks mercilessly. Every accusation in our life starts first with Satan.

Then I heard a loud voice saying in Heaven, "Now salvation, and strength, and the kingdom of our God, and the power of His Christ

*have come, for the accuser of our brethren, who accused them before
our God day and night, has been cast down.*
~ **Rev. 12:10**

Satan is full of evil, darkness and deception. Devil is *diabolos* in Greek, which means slanderer or false accuser. We cannot be blind to this. Our eyes must be opened to the true fight of deception. One of the biggest lies the accuser is capable of is coming as the angel of light. Satan, the devil, the angel of light? Seriously? Yes. If we don't recognize who and what he is, we can be deceived.

And no wonder!
For Satan himself transforms himself into an angel of light.
~ **II Cor. 11:14**

This first chapter will lay a foundation of who the accuser is, traits we may come to recognize and what characteristics we should be aware of. Some of us, never sensing the presence of the accuser, makes his job easier; we don't bother to question his lies to see if they are even the truth or not. Recognizing what is happening in our daily lives, in our conversations and our relationships with others, will help us to not be drawn in and baited by the true accuser.

I would like to point out here when describing the accuser in the next pages if we recognize these traits in a person we know and may be dealing with this type of situation with him or her right now, this is not saying the devil is in this person. We can all be used by the enemy of our soul that is not saying someone is possessed by the devil. This book is to bring knowledge and with that knowledge, the blessing of all of us growing in the Lord Jesus Christ.

For we wrestle not against flesh and blood, but against principalities, against powers, against the rulers of the darkness of this world, against spiritual wickedness in high places.

~ Ephesians 6:12

The accuser may be masquerading as many things; he can come with what sounds like our own thoughts, using our own voice. He can use an acquaintance, a friend, a family member, a fellow employee, a fellow church member and any other creative outlet that he can find.

It seems normal if the accuser, the enemy of our soul, is trying to lie to us in our mind; but if the accuser is someone close to us, that just doesn't seem possible or right. When the true accuser uses that course of action to get at us, it can feel like it causes more emotional hurt.

The damage of the accuser is the same, no matter what form it comes in. If we believe his accusations, then we are believing his lies. The accuser can only tell lies. The accuser's work is to destroy; so whatever we are dealing with, we can still be hurt; we can still be hindered in our purpose for God. We can still fall into guilt, shame and blame; and more important, think of all the time we waste trying to get over the accusations or clear our name. We could have been doing something purposeful towards the destiny that God has for us. Remember, the true accuser doesn't want to make himself known; he just wants to keep us busy in everything but our Father's business.

The accuser accuses, plain and simple. The accuser imputes guilt or blame. Accusers want their accusations to make believers out of us that we have done something wrong. They want us to feel at fault, regardless if we are or not. In situations, an accuser will hold someone else responsible for all the bad, all the time. In the accusations, one of the accuser's goals is wanting to see that person punished for his or her shortcomings.

An accuser criticizes everything nothing or no one measures up. Accusers will find fault with everything. We will find the accuser belittling everyone. The accuser believes we have failed them. When in a conversation with an accuser, he will be negative, slamming, whining and slashing to a fault.

The accuser can devalue a person in a moment. We will not find the accuser talking in a positive manner about anything. Just a few words spoken in a negative way from the accuser can plant the seed of implication, causing doubt, and now the accusation has started.

Implication: Something that is implied. A suggestion. Leading conclusion. An accusation that is understood without being spoken. An incriminating involvement.

The accuser is recognized as the informer, also known as the biggest whistleblower. The accusers' goal is to report, make known, and gossip about all they know. Knowing something private would not stay private with accusers; there is a need in them to supply the news and to find fault. The accuser actually loves taking credit for being the source. The accuser is proud to bring something into the open. They must promote someone else's shortcomings.

We can rest assured the accuser is waiting for someone to mess up. Accusers also try to bait their prey. They seem to have a gift for making the innocent talk in a conversation with them. The accuser is talented in drawing a person into a gossip-type conversation, making the unaware person an accomplice in the accusations.

Accomplice: one associated with another especially in wrongdoing. Abettor, cohort.

The accuser is well known as the double-crosser, the tattletale and the rat. Loving to accuse, ratting someone else out in a situation is the accusers' norm. They want to have influence and power. Accusers need someone to blame in all things. By blaming, they feel superior. They need to be the tattler because by doing so, they are showing who the less-worthy are; and by pointing out the faults of others, that makes the accusers "perfect."

Accusers are good at what they do and may even enjoy the controversy they stir up. For some accusers, accusing is their life; it is what gives them the excitement and fulfillment in what is missing. They enjoy spreading the hurt and stirring up trouble.

Since the norm for accusers is not to make themselves known, they use simple interjections into every conversation they are part of. They are sneaky. We will hear their words; and before we even know it, their accusations are planted in our minds. Most of the time, we won't even recognize we have heard an accusation from them. They are subtle. Clever. I like to call an accuser the bad sower or seed planter. Their accusations can slander, hide the truth and cause irreparable damage.

There is no mercy with an accuser. The accuser will back bite in a vulture-like manner. Accusers will distort the facts to fit their need to criticize. Their purpose for their attack is to destroy to weaken the reputation. Past mistakes and poor decisions will be used to fault find. If we have found ourselves dealing with accusers, it will be difficult, if not impossible, to defend ourselves against them. The truth will be hard to convince, once accusers have planted their conniving lies.

I want to point out here that I truly believe in focusing on the good things of the Kingdom Realm of God, *not* focusing on what the enemy sends into our daily walk; but we truly need to be aware of the accusers and what they may be up to. Knowledge of the devices, tactics and tricks the accuser could be using is beneficial to us. He is the father of lies; we cannot believe one thing he says or does. Having this knowledge of recognition will help us to prepare and be ready and dodge anything he has for us.

In the following chapters, we will look at the ways of the accuser and what we can do to separate ourselves from the accuser's tactics. We will learn spiritual awareness and training. We are soldiers for the Lord, and He has a game plan that works. Let's follow it!

~ CHAPTER 1 REVIEW ~

- The accuser may be masquerading as many things. In what ways have you recognized this in your own life?

- An accuser criticizes everything nothing or no one measures up. In what ways have you found yourself dealing with accusations from the accuser?

How Do We Miss It?

We have an idea who the accuser is now, so how do we miss it? How are we so unaware some times of his devices? How can we be so blind? How could we be so deceived by the accuser and listen to him? We ask ourselves how we believed the lies. How do others believe the lies about us that an accuser tells them?

The accuser is a sly fox. Remember, he doesn't want to make himself known, so he interjects randomly into our lives a little here and a little there. Every day, it is his goal to blind us to his tactics and trip us, so we stumble along not knowing what hit us. If he can keep us scrambling and defending ourselves all day, he did what he wanted to do.

How do we miss the accuser in our mind? I think we miss him because he tries to sound like our own voice, or he comes in the voice of someone close to us. He reminds us of what maybe someone close to us said many years ago, and then he uses his or her voice as if it is today. What was said may not have been kind or uplifting in the past, so he brings that back to us and tries to rub it in our face. Yes, someone may have said the accusations to us years ago, but it is the accuser who is reminding us now. He wants to take away; he wants us to be defeated before we even start. And because it was from our past, we don't identify it is the accuser who is saying it now.

Most of us know what our own faults are, so the accuser can remind us in our own voice. He doesn't have to get fancy here. He will bring up our shortcomings, the ones we have an issue with, and sound just like ourselves, which makes it easier for us to believe the accusations. He gets us to believe we are thinking it; and by thinking it, we believe the accusations about ourselves again, and they are renewed as a fresh fault we can feel guilty about once again.

Does this sound familiar? "Yeah, I couldn't do that. Yeah, I failed at that. Yeah, I was really scared to do that." Yeah, yeah, yeah equals lie, lie, lie.

Does this mean some of our thoughts are not our own? Right! When negativity, fear and guilt try to overcome us, we can guess who is busy at work. Replace every lie with the positive goodness from the word of God. We need to take control over all the thoughts that are not ours. Don't claim them. Even if the accuser uses what we believe was the truth of our past, they are lies to us now because we have been forgiven by the blood of Jesus Christ. That is what we need to claim!

I want to focus on interjections here because we need to learn what they are. From my experience, the interjections into our mind or from a person can be so glossed over maybe even graceful like. Our mind just sort of dances with them for a second. Then they get us before we know we've been had. The interjection was said so simply, out of the blue; and we're not sure we even heard it right. We even question the implication of the interjection. But it is an interjection to plant the deceiving seed into our minds. Once planted, the influence is now there to cause doubt on whatever subject the interjection was about.

If we have been weak in an area in the past, let's say fear, we will hear thoughts like this, for example;

- You can't.
- You don't deserve that.
- You could never do that.
- Do you want to fail again?
- It wasn't meant to be.
- Do you want people to know you aren't capable?
- What will people think?
- You know what happened the last time.
- Do you really want to make a fool out of yourself?
- Why do you think you should do that?
- Who told you to do that?

These kind of negative thoughts will go on and on in our minds when the accuser is present or when we have taken on where the accuser has left off. Interjections are what they are. Every time we are blessed, the accuser will tell us we don't deserve it. The accuser tries to take every happy moment from our lives. He wants us to be deprived of all spiritual power to overcome.

The accuser will use our past against us; his memory is good and he doesn't forget. God has forgiven our sins and will not remember them, but the accuser remembers them and wants to remind us on a daily basis. Our past is exactly that, the past. It happened; we can learn from it and we can use it to the glory of the Lord. Good or bad, it is yesterday, and we need to live in today. We should not let the accuser ever use it against us.

I, even I, am he that blotteth out thy transgressions for mine own sake, and will not remember thy sins.

~ Isaiah 43:25

If our past is not enough for the accuser, he will use our today, our right now. He will try to mess up our day, so we get nothing done in our Kingdom purpose or grow in our Kingdom destiny. The fiery darts will come in random ways, and I will go as far to say, funny ways, meaning we should never have cared about them in the first place. But they are not funny when we believe them, and they hurt us.

We go to pay a bill, and then the money fear thoughts go off like crazy in our mind. Or the phone rings and as we move to answer it, we wonder who is calling and is something wrong. Two to three wild, crazy, doom and gloom thoughts go through our mind before we have even reached the phone, and it was only a telemarketer. Been there?

How about this one? We feel a pain or an ache, and the name of every fatal disease races through our mind with horrible fear. It grips us for days. Some of us may even go to the doctor for fear of what the ache is, and we are as healthy as an ox. I'm not saying here if something really is making us feel bad not to go to the doctor, I am talking about living in constant fear of an illness. Many of us have been healed by God and are still living in fear because the accuser keeps reminding us of the disease we did have, and he threatens us every day that it is coming back. We need to be wise and take care of the body God gave us, but listening to the accuser has to stop; we need to walk in our healings and promises of God.

I love this one because at the very start of our day the accuser shows up did you know that just getting dressed in the morning can be major spiritual warfare for many? As we look in our closets to see what we should put on for our day, the thoughts start. We think we don't have any clothes and we have a closet full: we don't own a tie to go with the new dress shirt; all our dress pants are old; we have nothing to wear; all our dresses are out of style. Then the thoughts start that we wouldn't look good in any of them anyway: we are too fat; we are too skinny; we are…we are…we are what?

What is the accuser trying to do? Do we recognize any of this as our early morning routines? Then all the mental pictures start of what we aren't. We aren't this; we aren't that; we're not the right image; we won't live up. These interjections would wear the average person out before his or her day started. Before we know it, our whole morning has changed, but we were fine when we stepped out of the bed. The accuser gets us off focus of who we are we are the child of the King. A very important person to the Lord.

Does any of this really happen? Yes and daily. That is what I call the accuser's interjections.

Interjection - means an abrupt comment put in the middle of a sentence, a short utterance added, an emotional word added, the act of uttering suddenly, emotional remarks, bursts of uttering.

I picture the accuser as this little, evil dark thing, shooting very little darts (interjections) –and those by themselves can't really do anything. But if we let him, the darts can do a huge amount of damage to us. That is the key, *if* we let him.

The old saying we can be our own worst enemy is true. We need to be aware of what we are saying to ourselves. We need to focus and listen to those thoughts. Where are they coming from? Are we insecure in who we are? Are we beating ourselves up and doing the accuser's job? Are we forgetting God's promises and letting our faith go to weak levels?

Many of us have believed the accuser's words for so long that we have taken on where he has left off. Again, the accuser is sneaky; once he has gotten us to believe what he has told us, he knows we will walk in the shame of his accusations. But we serve a mighty God who loosens the chains of accusations, who delivers us from their fear, who reaches into the miry clay and brings us out; and above all, our God will restore unto us what the accuser has taken away. In the future chapters, we will explore how we can take back our thoughts and reign them in to God's way. God loves us and wants to protect our thoughts.

The next way the accuser will try to deceive is in our future. Our tomorrows and our future haven't even happened yet, but the accuser can be and probably is already there waiting for us. His purpose is that we don't have a future, and we don't have a tomorrow. He would be happy if we stayed in the past reliving, all of our yesterdays and not moving forward.

God has given each of us dreams. He believes in us. Some of us may have already seen the future in our mind; we have seen with clarity what God sees for us, and we have seen our destiny in Him. That is God's goal for us--that His plan has become our dream and destiny, too.

As we reach for those goals and dreams, the accuser will want to steal them from us. He does not want us to succeed and believe in them.

The accuser does not want us to trust in God with our tomorrows. The accuser wants to shut us down, blind us on the path and stop us at all cost. He wants to steal our future because he knows his future!

As we begin to see the path for our tomorrows unfold, the accuser will bring up all the reasons why it will never happen. He will attack every step we take. As we put the action into our faith of seeing a goal we are moving to attain, this is when we must be ready to dodge the accusations of the accuser. The accuser will try to get us off focus of moving forward. His goal will be to plant anything that would weaken us to set a solid course of action in what we know to do. Of course, this is something we should not listen to. We have to stop letting him in our tomorrows. He will try to discourage us from making any dream happen; and for many of us, he has tried and has had some success already. But we can stop this pattern in our life!

Take therefore no thought for the morrow:
for the morrow shall take thought for the things of itself.
~ Matthew 6:34

You will not need to fight in this battle. Position yourselves, stand still and see the salvation of the Lord, who is with you, O Judah and Jerusalem! Do not fear or be dismayed; tomorrow go out against them, for the Lord is with you.
~ II Chronicles 20:17

For I know the thoughts that I think toward you, says the Lord, thoughts of peace and not of evil, to give you a future and a hope.
~ Jeremiah 29:11

Peace I leave with you, My peace I give to you; not as the world gives do I give to you. Let not your heart be troubled, neither let it be afraid.

~ John 14:27

How do we miss the accuser when it is a person? Again, I think for the most part, we are unaware of the behavior of an accuser because we want to think good of people. We want to give people the benefit of the doubt. We don't want to believe that someone could be saying something bad about anyone. We want to think the best, even if we are in the middle of a true accusing situation. When the accuser is coming in the way of a person, the accusations are just as damaging. This betrayal can feel worse; and especially if it's from people we know and love, the hurt can be overwhelming. The shock alone can take a long time to get over. Then we have to deal with what the accusations were. The hurt is meant to destroy us, and it is from the true accuser.

We can go on for a while and still not recognize the danger of this kind of behavior. If the person is accusing us with interjections that keep us down, attacks our self-esteem, or makes us not believe, it could take years of defending ourselves before we see it could be useless. We can waste precious time if we are unaware of the obstacles in our life. Negativity and blame will hinder us from moving forward like we should. If the interjections are daily or on a regular basis, we will take one step forward and two steps back trying to overcome them.

If we are privy to accusers saying something about other people, I do believe the same feelings apply. We don't want to think badly about them. We want to give them the benefit of the doubt. Maybe they just need to unload and they are trusting us with this, so we listen.

We don't want to believe they could be saying what we think they are saying. We want to think well of them and not face what is actually happening. Many times here, if we are honest with ourselves, we know we are hearing something not right about someone else.

When the accuser is talking bad about someone to us, while we may still be clueless of the damage because we want to think good of this person, the destroying damage is still going on. Accusers can paint a destructive image of the person they are talking about; and by hearing this, we will be influenced.

Remember, accusers want to plant bad seeds about whom they are finding fault with. They want to punish and condemn them. Once we hear the distorted facts in our minds, we will have to overcome that influence to think right about that person again. If we start to believe the conniving lies, it will be difficult to see the truth. And now, we are deceived about someone else, who cannot defend themselves. A good piece of wisdom here is: the accuser is usually the guilty party of all they accuse.

I would like to point out, there are times people will have to talk to someone or be counseled in a situation about someone. They will have to talk about the facts of a person and what they are dealing with; this is not what I am referring to here. There will be a chapter further on covering if the accuser we are battling with is a person.

Either way, in our mind or with a person, knowing and recognizing the accuser's tactics will help us to come back with the word of God and claim our purposed future. We do not have to worry if we have felt the accuser in our tomorrows, accusing and trying to take. We can change all of that right now by becoming more aware. We are as we read these pages; we will have victory!

We need to protect what God has for us. We need to wake up to whom the accuser is and how important it is to recognize the ways of the accuser of the brethren. God has a plan for each of us and a purpose. God is in our tomorrows already protecting them.

~ CHAPTER 2 REVIEW ~

- The accuser is a sly fox. Remember, he doesn't want to make himself known, so he interjects randomly into our lives—a little here and a little there. How have you missed the accuser in the past?

- An accuser uses interjections into our everyday life. Do you recognize any interjections in your life?

Our Past Sins

As a believer, our past sins are forgiven by our Lord Jesus Christ. But when the true accuser reminds us of them again and again with his incriminating words—then sometimes we have a hard time believing that they are forgiven. The memories of them seem to pop up in our mind at the strangest and weakest times. This is not by accident. We are in a spiritual warfare to do what is right and be who we are in Christ. Moving in a forward direction and growing in God makes us a prime candidate for the enemy of our soul's attention.

Be sober, be vigilant; because your adversary the devil, as a roaring lion, walks about, seeking whom he may devour:

~ 1 Peter 5:8

What does accusing and reminding us of our past sins do to us? Well, it can do a lot, actually. We can experience a setback in our Christian growth. If we are consistently battling the past and not moving forward, and beyond our forgiven sins, then we are swimming against the tide and not getting anywhere. As we are being reminded and accused of our past, we can also relive the guilt, shame, and blame of those forgiven sins.

By reliving, we are *living* them. As we become aware of whom the accuser is, we can also recognize the damaging effect the accuser is trying to do by bringing up our old sinful past. When our mind and thoughts are attacked with this, then our daily life is affected also.

Looking at the emotions and feelings we experience will also help us see where and how the accuser comes into our lives. For example, one of the common emotions we can feel is guilt.

Guilt—is the feeling of remorsefulness, the state of having done something wrong, self-reproach, inadequacy and feeling responsible for the bad.

Our past sins, even though forgiven, can bring these feelings back up when we are listening to the accuser. We can thank God we felt remorseful for our past sins, and we have gone to the throne of Jesus for forgiveness; but that is where we should leave them.

Because we are human, it does take time to walk in our forgiveness and get out from under those past feelings of guilt. If we are still experiencing this because we are a new Christians, we need to give ourselves some time. If we are still experiencing this forgiveness as a new babe in Christ, this is not the time to beat ourselves up. The goal is to walk forward in our forgiveness; because if we have confessed our sins, than He is faithful to forgive them.

Blame is another feeling of emotion we will re-experience when reliving our past sins. Although forgiven we can start blaming ourselves all over again for a deed that has been taken care of by the blood of Jesus Christ.

Blame—is being the cause of something, at fault, responsible of the act, deserving of punishment, condemn, criticize, and denounced.

Walking in the blame of the accuser will make us expect bad things. When our liberty and freedom in our walk with God's forgiveness is being attacked by the accuser's lies, it will feel like there is a black cloud hanging over us. That black cloud will make us expect bad things in our lives. Our circumstances can be going along just fine, and then we find ourselves expecting something bad will happen. Instead of the good things of God, we are looking for something bad to happen to us.

The accuser can make us believe we don't deserve the good things of God. How far can we go if we don't believe in the good things of God, and instead we are walking in the emotional abuse of the accuser? We will not get far.

If we let the accuser make us believe we have not been set free, then all that the Lord has done for us is for naught. The feeling of unbelief will create all kinds of negative emotions in us.

Unbelief—is doubt, skepticism, lack of faith, mistrust; and all definitions of unbelief refer and lead to our unbelief in God.

For God so loved the world that he gave his one and only Son, that
whoever believes in him shall not perish but have eternal life.
~ John 3:16

We cannot limit Calvary. Calvary is finished. It is done. By confessing our sins and believing in whom God has sent, our Lord

Jesus Christ, who shed His blood for us, we have been set free and cleansed. We can go boldly to the throne of our forgiving Lord. And if we haven't asked God for forgiveness and claimed Him as our Savior, then we can right now!

If we confess our sins, he is faithful and just to forgive us our sins and to cleanse us from all unrighteousness.

~ 1 John 1:9

If we listen to the accuser, we will second guess everything. Guarding what we listen to is not a bad idea here. Holding conversations with the enemy of our souls is not profitable. Listening is an action on our part. We should not give the accuser an ear. We will discuss further on how we can go about that successfully.

Listening - is to make an effort to hear something, to pay attention, and to heed.

Once we have listened to the lies and paid attention to those bad seeds just planted in our minds, that will make us heed to them. Then we start the second-guessing.

Second-guessing—is to question a decision or an action that has already been done.

Do we see ourselves here? Once we start second guessing, we are not sure of anything anymore. We are not sure we can even count on our decisions. Then we become scared to make decisions. We no longer trust we are hearing from God; we get kind of foggy where God's voice is concerned. Having known God's voice in the past, we can become unsure which voice in our head is God's. Every right turn we begin to take, we wonder if we should have gone left. We feel scattered. Confused. Lost.

Amazing, how we were once found and no longer lost in Christ Jesus, and then we feel lost again. How does that happen? Especially since we were going along just fine, and then we find ourselves falling down this slippery slope to our past sins again. The accuser does not want us to walk forward on the path that God has for us; he would rather we trip up and start sliding downhill into his cunning lies. And better yet, we believe them.

Once we let doubt come in, especially to what God has done for us, who we are in God, we start wondering if our sins have been forgiven. This is a good sign we have listened to the accuser, and we are now second-guessing.

Doubt—is feeling uncertain, lack of conviction, to question, suspicious, suspect, distrust, mistrust, disbelieve, second guessing, fear, skeptical and unsettled.

The definition of doubt sounds so serious here; and if we put those different meanings into our relationship with God, it sounds even worse. Just look at what it does when we let doubt in because of the true accuser. We would never want to be guilty of truly suspecting or distrusting God would we?

Is allowing the accuser to bring that into our relationship meaning we are allowing it? I don't believe consciously any of us would want to do that. Again, let's pause here for a moment and reflect on the importance of knowing who the accuser is and what the accuser does because doubt is doubt. Doubt is a game changer in our faith. We can't have faith in something we doubt.

As we relive our sinful past and the accuser has tried to weaken us, he will play dirty and try to tempt us with our own past sins. Here we are forgiven, walking along in our lives of purpose, and then the accuser comes with a corrupt reminder. We don't see it coming, and then we've been hit. He reminds us, bringing it all back up again with scents, thoughts, pictures and feelings. He tempts us with the very thing he is accusing us with. Not a lot of imagination here. He is sly and cunning, but not something we can't overcome with the blood of Jesus.

For instance, let's say in our old, sinful life, we were a compulsive liar. As the accuser brings it back up in our face, and we let him, we start to feel bad. Then we start blaming ourselves again, which weakens us; and before we know it, we are tempted to lie to cover up what we are going through. The accuser doesn't have fancy tactics there at all but his tactics can work, if we let them. What a liar and tempter the accuser is, but we serve one better than that. And we can go boldly before our Lord and ask for His help. The past is exactly that, the past. Let us trust that God does not remind us of our past; and if He doesn't, we shouldn't let the accuser do it either.

Let us therefore come boldly unto the throne of grace, that we may obtain mercy, and find grace to help in time of need.

~ *Hebrews 4:16*

We can fill in the above, for instance, with anything. If we've had problems with drugs, alcohol, sexual issues or whatever that is what the accuser will bring back to use against us. Our believing in what God has forgiven us of and whom we are now in Jesus could become tainted with unbelief, if we allow the accuser to sway us; and that is opposite of whom we are in Christ. We are believers not unbelievers.

In the garden, with Adam and Eve, as soon as they sinned, they hid. Listening and talking with the enemy of their souls caused them to doubt what God had told them; and after they disobeyed, they felt guilt and shame, causing separation from God.

If we listen to the accuser, who by the way is not more powerful then what we have, just cunning and a liar, and let our past forgiven sins come back to make us feel guilty, bad and undeserving, we could hide from God, too.

And they heard the voice of the LORD God walking in the garden in the cool of the day: and Adam and his wife hid themselves from the presence of the LORD God amongst the trees of the garden.

~ Genesis 3:8

I think we pull back and hide because we try to fix ourselves alone. We try to get a handle on it, before we want to go to God. The shame at being tempted and falling short in our estimation could keep us from God because we feel guilty. We begin to think we can't go to God now—what is He going to think of us? We feel the shame that we should not be in this predicament at all.

We can fall into the trap that is set for us and think there is something wrong with us if we are letting these past sins back into our lives. We then start to second-guess. The doubting and the blaming can really snag us. Once we have our feet tangled in the accuser's lies and we take over where the accuser has left off, we allow our blunders to make us feel undeserving of God's forgiveness. Then the accuser did his work on us, didn't he? He got us hiding from God.

That is all he wants to do, too. He doesn't have to come with a shout and get the big guns out to make himself known. He doesn't even have to put up a huge fight to destroy us, just enough to get us hiding because his number one goal is to keep us from God.

I believe for the most part a lot of us do not realize the accuser is lurking around because he doesn't come at us with some kind of huge offense in our lives. If it is the enemy of our souls, we picture bigger things, scary things happening to us. Depending on our imaginations, we could think he'd only come at us in dark and evil sinister ways, which could happen; but most every day, fiery darts from the enemy of our soul are on the smaller level and go undetected. Under the radar, low blows are his best work. If we aren't aware of him, we don't know how to fight or pray.

If we are dealing with a person who accuses us with our past sins and we let that weaken our confidence in what God has done for us, then that can be the destructive thing in our lives. We can find ourselves not going around other people who may know about what they are saying; we can second guess our forgiveness; we can doubt;

we can be weakened trying to defend ourselves, and it is usually a big waste of time defending what God has done for us to this person. We can get so caught up defending a past that has already been forgiven. Wasting a lot of time being busy with defending is a tactic of the accuser also.

We do not have to walk in shame of our past sins and shortcomings. We have victory over them by the blood of Jesus Christ! Our testimony is powerful. That is why the accuser wants to take it away. If we help others overcome their past sins by the testimony of our faith and victories, we advance the Kingdom of God, which is exactly what the accuser does not want to happen.

~ CHAPTER 3 REVIEW ~

- What does accusing and reminding us of our past sins do to us? Well, it can do a lot, actually. We can experience a setback in our Christian growth. Though, we are forgiven, how can this be a setback if you listen?

- Walking in the blame of the accuser will make us expect bad things. Have you found yourself expecting bad things and in what way?

The Falsely Accused in the Bible

P ride, jealously, envy and selfishness seem to be the root reasons for false accusations in the stories from the Bible. From the beginning of time people have suffered from false accusations.

Ninth Commandment—You shall not bear false witness against your neighbor.

Moses and Aaron—In the book of Numbers 16, they are falsely accused by Korah of taking too much upon themselves. We can read of Korah's rebellion and punishment in that chapter, and we read there how God told Moses and Aaron to separate themselves from the congregation.

Moses—Moses was accused and was looked down upon by his own sister and brother. Miriam and Aaron accused Moses of being full of himself and usurping the authority given to him. The Lord heard what they said to Moses, and He had something to say about that.

The Lord called the three of them out unto the tabernacle, and then the Lord's anger was kindled against Miriam and Aaron. The scripture says Moses was a meek man, above all men on the face of the earth. I like to think that was mentioned because what Miriam and Aaron were trying to accuse Moses of was not true; and by accusing him of that, it was obvious it was a lie and meant for evil. Read their story and punishment in Numbers 12.

Jeremiah –The Prophet of God is falsely accused of wishing to desert to the enemy and was imprisoned. Read this story in Jeremiah 37.

Joseph - Joseph was falsely accused by Potiphar's wife. She did not get what she wanted from Joseph, so she lied and accused, wanting him punished. In his punishment, God showed him mercy and gave him favor with the keeper of the prison. What the enemy meant for harm, God changed to good. Read this story in Genesis 39.

Daniel—Daniel was falsely accused over jealousy when no fault could be found in him. He was then thrown in the lion's den. The Lord sent an angel to close the mouth of the lion, and he was released. All those that were jealous, with their families, were thrown in the lion's den by the King. God took care of the false accusations again. Read this story in Daniel 6.

Job—Job's three friends accused him of being a sinner. In their minds, he had to be, because of all of the bad things that were happening to him. In God's eyes, Job was perfect and upright. Read this story in the book of Job.

David—David was falsely accused by his brother, right before his battle with Goliath a great story of wonderful wisdom for all of us. David turned away from his brother's accusing words and moved in the direction God was pointing him in. Read this story starting in 1 Samuel 17:28.

Jesus—Jesus said the Son of Man was accused of being a drunkard and gluttonous in the book of Matthew 11:19. Read in Mark 14 where many tried to bare false witness against Jesus, but none of their stories agreed to be right. As the chef priests accused him of many things, Jesus stayed silent.

These are just a few examples for us to learn from. We can read throughout the Bible where the people of God have been falsely accused. Their testimonies are to encourage us and remind us we are not alone, and we stand with a wonderful, righteous lot of people. The one thing we can count on is God hears it all, and He will take care of it!

Blessed are you when others revile you and persecute you and utter all kinds of evil against you falsely on my account.
~ Matthew 5: 11

Having a good conscience, so that when you are slandered, those who revile your good behavior in Christ may be put to shame.
~ 1 Peter 3:16

*The Pharisees and the teachers of the law were
looking for a reason to accuse Jesus, so they watched him closely
to see if he would heal on the Sabbath.*

~ Luke 6:7

*But realize this, that in the last days, difficult times will come. For men
will be lovers of self, lovers of money, boastful, arrogant, revilers,
disobedient to parents, ungrateful, unholy, unloving, irreconcilable,
malicious gossips, without self-control, brutal, haters of good,
treacherous, reckless, conceited, lovers of pleasure rather than lovers
of God, holding to a form of godliness, although they have denied its
power; Avoid such men as these.*

~ II Timothy 3:1-5

*Having a good conscience, that when they defame you as evildoers,
those who revile your good conduct in Christ may be ashamed.*

~ I Peter 3:16

~ CHAPTER 4 REVIEW ~

- The falsely accused are many in the Bible. Do you find yourself relating to any and why?

Accusing People

I n the first few chapters, we have read about the definition of the word, accuser. We also know from the scriptures who accuses us daily before God. But in this chapter we will solely focus on people who may accuse us falsely.

We may not be surprised, and it may feel somewhat expected if we recognize the accuser's voice as the enemy of our soul. But when it is a person, the accusations and the hurt can cut like a knife because we don't want to believe someone we know could do that to us. It can be a crushing blow when it is someone we love and really care about.

From my experiences and the experiences of others who have shared with me, I do believe we are falsely accused by people a lot more than we care to admit or believe. I am not trying to look for trouble here, nor should you; but I do believe we need to be aware of this, so we are not walking in condemnation, guilt and the blame that will hinder us doing the will of God in our lives.

Again, it is our innate belief that we want to believe the good in people. Also, another point here, if we do not falsely accuse people ourselves, we will not necessarily recognize people who falsely accuse us or others. It follows along with the principal: if you are not a manipulator, you may not recognize a manipulator; if you are not a criminal, you may not recognize criminal behavior. The same goes if our normal behavior is not being a false accuser or a blamer, we may not recognize that kind of behavior in others right away.

Let's go over some basic examples of dealing with an accuser in our daily lives. We could have been a victim of this for years; this is totally new to us; or we've just experienced something like this recently.

As a child, we could have experienced this from a parent, a teacher, a family member or a friend. For instance, a parent could have blamed us regularly for things we did or did not do or in areas of our life that did not measure up to what they wanted out of us.

A teacher could have pegged us totally wrong from the first day of school, and we could never get out of that false reputation they put on us. Our childhood friends could have accused us instead of fessing up themselves for a bad deed done or accused us of personality traits that may or may not be true, and they are still hindering us today.

In a lot of these situations, we could not have done a thing to defend ourselves for the most part. We were young and who would have believed us? How do we stand up to a parent? We usually don't stand up to a parent because we only want him or her to love us and his or her opinion means the most to us. How could we change a teacher's opinion of us, when we didn't even know what we did to become so pegged? Lies from friends are hard to prove unless we have witnesses that come to our defense.

As a child, I was accused of stealing one of my grandmother's rings by her husband (who was not my grandfather). I was devastated. I loved my grandmother very much and would not have stolen anything from her or anyone else for that matter. I thank God she believed in me, but I had no proof. My grandmother waited until her husband left the house the day after I was accused, and then she searched all of the pockets in his clothes in the closet. In one of his suit jackets, my grandmother found the missing ruby ring. I was so relieved, but the accusation stuck. I was hurt and actually shocked that someone would do that to me. My grandmother believed he was jealous of her love for me and did that to make me look bad in her eyes. I was grateful in that situation because of my grandmother's belief in me and her finding the ring, but I've never forgotten how I felt being falsely accused.

I was accused of stealing and not to take away from that—because it scared me and hurt me—but I knew I *did not* steal anything. What of words that hurt and accuse, like we are dumb, stupid, uncompassionate, uncaring and many more? Words hurt even when untrue. I think words of character or personality traits may hurt us more because we may not be sure or have the confidence that the words of the accuser are untrue. When I was accused of stealing and my grandmother believed in me, it was easier for me to get over this because I *knew* I was not a thief, and I had her trust.

But how many of us are not so lucky? Accusations that are not true, hurt. We may still hear the voices of our youth right now as we are reading this…the teacher who said we weren't smart; the parent who cussed their accusations at us instead of blessing us and the children of our youth, whom we thought were friends, but name called, laughed, teased and accused us. These kinds of accusations could have shaped our first years and could still be influencing us right now. As we study this and remember any hurts from the past, please take note of them for future reference and give them to the Lord.

At the workplace, an accuser can make our lives miserable. Our jobs are so important to our lives. It is our livelihood; plus we are there for hours, so working with someone who is trying to throw us under the bus, so to speak, can become stressful. Defending ourselves and the pressure of watching our backs can be all-consuming. An accusing co-worker can make our job almost unbearable.

When we find out that a friend or someone very close to us is accusing us of things that we did not do or would never plan to do, it is like a cold blast to the heart. I think again here the first thing we feel is shock. We don't want to believe it. We reason with ourselves it can't be possible.

If we have given this person our trust, maybe our love, it is even harder to believe he or she could have done something like this to us. The accusations could have come through the accuser, or we've been told or heard from another reliable source either way we may not know how to defend ourselves or how to deal with it.

If we have been falsely accused and the accuser is going around spewing the accusations and gossiping to everyone we know, our first inclination is to defend ourselves. We want to jump right in and call everyone to tell our side of the story. Our heart beats wild at the lies; we can't sleep under the falsehoods out there about us. We feel the shame of the falsehood, and we want so much to get the truth out there. We feel betrayed, alone and confused. We worry about who may believe the accuser. We wonder how we are going to get our side of the story told.

Accusers will tell anyone who will listen—that we are this or we are that. We are not compassionate; we are not there for them; we have ruined their lives; we are to blame for everything wrong in their lives; we did this or we did that; we caused their sickness; we are threatening them somehow; we are punishing them and we are out to get them.

None of this is true, in most situations; but the one thing I have found to be true and I will say again is accusers in all falsehoods are usually guilty of all that they accuse. *They* are not compassionate; they are not there for others; they have ruined their own lives; they are to blame for the wrongs; they have caused their own sicknesses; they are threatening; they want to punish and they are out to get someone. Out of their own mouths are their hearts.

Now, when we have heard these accusations against us, again, our first reaction usually is to want to respond. When Jesus was accused, he said nothing. When David was accused, he prayed to God to fight his battles. We can see through history that our best response could be not to respond, but to pray.

Believe me, I know we may have wanted to pick up the phone, make a Facebook post and meet with every friend or family member we are sure who knows what this accuser is saying about us, but what good would it do? We could lower ourselves to the accuser's level, which I do believe he or she wants us to do. We should not give their condemning words a lot of attention. Not giving attention to the blaming words may not make the person stop, but it will help us not to waste time in living our purposed life.

Another point I would like to share is when dealing with an accusing person we want to separate ourselves from—for example, after getting to know someone better and we sense he or she talks bad about people and accuse, we may even know the person talks bad about us—and not wanting any part of that kind of behavior in our relationships, we try to move on. If the person is an accuser, he or she will recognize what we are doing and that will stir the accuser up against us even more. Again, not trying to look for trouble here, but I have seen this happen again and again. Our relationship with an accuser could get worse before it gets better.

Once accusers know we know who they are and what they are up to, they may try to make us look bad anyway they can, because we are a threat to them. If they were accusing us of things before, they will get worse; and if they weren't accusing us before, just talking about others to us, then they will start accusing us now. The reason for that is they do not want to be known; accusers cannot stand when they are found out, so now they must ruin, blame and try to destroy our reputations.

If we have confronted an accuser, we will see the same kind of behavior. Confronting an accuser is like stirring up a hornet's nest. We could have the best intentions in going to the accuser. We care for this person, and we want him or her to know we did not do what he or she is accusing us of; or we think if we confront an accuser in love, we may be able to fix the situation, change the outcome and help. This could create a bigger problem than we had before.

Pinning accusers down and trying to fix the lies they have told usually ends up in bigger accusations from them. Most accusers do not believe their falsehoods are lies; they believe them to be the truth. They will not look in the mirror, nor will they see that they are doing anything wrong. By confronting them, we have made them go in to a protection mode *their* protection mode. We did it. We are to blame.

We are the guilty party, not them. We need to pay. Again, their behavior does not change. We could get in deeper and deeper with someone like this, and we could get more hurt and troubled by just trying to fix it.

Accusers won't stay with the truth. Remember their truth is lies. They will turn every conversation around until we are questioning ourselves and our motives. They are talented in getting the focus off of them and back onto us or others; someone else is always to blame.

When we are using wisdom, and our goal in our relationship with them is to try and set up some kind of boundaries, it is amazing how they will sense and know this. I have seen this happen again and again in situations. It is like someone or something is feeding them this information. We should not be surprised if they try to latch on worse to us or start accusing us more. It will feel like a no-win situation.

In a way, it is a no-win situation for those who do not want to listen and reconcile; but if we give it to the Lord and let Him fight the battle, if we stay away from the trouble they want to stir up and we stay quiet, not giving them something more to cause chaos with, I do believe we win. We win to go on; we win being a child of the Lord; and more important, we let God have control over the situation, and He will take care of it! It is a win-win for us.

Most of us will have some kind of concern when dealing with the people acting as accusers because we care for their lives, their souls and their person. Do not be troubled, but walk in the peace of God because our testimony, our behavior, our forgiveness and our prayers for them may be used when their hearts are ready for a change. But only the Lord can truly help them. They must want the help of the

Lord, so leave it in His hands. We cannot expect to help them if they are not asking for God's help. If this sounds harsh, I write this because most of the time we are pulled back in. We think we can help them. And a lot of the times, we are acting not because God has asked us to, but because we don't want to let go and let God. By not letting God, we could get ourselves into more chaos and more hurt. We truly cannot force God's help on someone who does not want it.

If we are the ear for the accusers when they are accusing someone else, we must be careful here. We've touched on this subject earlier, but it is worth saying again. When we are the ear, we will be swayed by what the accuser is saying. We may think we are just trying to be kind or be a friend to the accuser, while that may be true, we should use extreme caution here because we are providing an ear.

One of the traps that we can fall into is thinking we are helping the accusers in some way by standing up for whom they are accusing. Trying to be positive and bring out the good about whom they are accusing is a normal first response from us. We think we can sway them. I do believe in the sincerity of our hearts, we really believe this, and that is why we can find ourselves in uncomfortable and tight situations with accuser-type people. We can go on and on until we are out of breath and blue in the face, but we've missed the most important thing here in our concern to help.

The accusers do not want any help. Nor have they asked us for any. That is a key to keep for a guideline in the future: has this person asked for our help or for God's help? Most of the time we will find they've never asked for help; we were the ones who thought we could help.

The accusing-type people usually want to turn us against whom they are talking about. They want to plant enough accusations that we will believe what they are saying. Their influence is their power. Their lies and interjections about whom they are accusing will plant bad seeds in our minds. If we listen we will start to believe the lies, even if we think we aren't. We will be the ones who are swayed, not them.

The focus will no longer be on their unkind words; the focus will be on whom they accused. Even if we did not believe their words in the beginning, their accusations will cause doubt. Once doubt is planted in our minds, we are open to the lie. We only have to hear something a few times for doubt to start its process. Once doubt is planted, we are doubting the truth.

What's worse, the accuser could get us to start accusing— gossiping about a LIE. I've seen where the accusers get people to believe the victims of their accusations brought it on themselves. The victims were too good of friends with the accusers; they should have known better; or the victims should never have told the accuser such things about their lives. They can get us even thinking what could the accusers have done? Then we begin to think the victims trusted them with too much information about their lives and brought this on themselves.

Amazing how the accusers can convince us the victims "did it". The victims were the bad people to get the accusers to talk about them: This *is the lie* we can be convinced to believe.

The victim is the innocent party. He or she trusted, liked and maybe even loved the accuser. Maybe they were friends, but once the

45

accuser became jealous… bam. All they shared in the friendship now has given the jealous accuser ammunition.

Maybe the victim was a co-worker and trusted her boss; but now the boss is threatened by her, so the accusations start. Or maybe the victim is a family member who simply loves his family, but another family member who is jealous of him is the accuser, who knows much and will twist and turn everything.

The innocent victims should not be looked down upon because they were open in a relationship with the accusers and trusted them. The focus when dealing with this type of situation needs to be put back on the accusers. Victims should not have to defend themselves in any way. The accuser is doing wrong, period.

We must recognize the accusers in these types of situations, and we must not be an ear to their accusations of others. We must not be swayed and influenced by lies. When dealing with an accuser who does not want to clear things up and change, we will get to the place called Nowhere with them. Our trying to help will not get us one step closer to a good ending, but two steps backwards every time we try. We could hear more, be hurt more, be affected more by the negativity, and in the end, have one huge hole we may have to dig ourselves out of.

The main destructiveness when dealing with accusers is what bad seed did they plant in us? What did the accusations about someone else or ourselves truly do to us? We won't walk away untouched.

We will be affected to some level by accusations about others or ourselves. If the accusations were about us, it will take some time to get over. It may take a very long time for some of us to get it out of our minds and not believe the accusations, especially if they were on a personal level and not an action we never did. If we have heard accusations about others, it will be the same. It could hinder our relationship with them and their reputation in our mind for days, and maybe even years.

We can see the importance of having this knowledge to help stop the accuser's work in our lives. We do not need this type of deception in our minds or our lives. God is here for us to wipe the slate clean. He can renew our minds and cleanse our hearts. All we need to do is ask for His help!

~ CHAPTER 5 REVIEW ~

- The true accuser doesn't surprise us with his behavior, but when dealing with an accusing person it is a different story. If dealing with an accusing person, how can this affect you?

- One of the traps that we can fall into is thinking we are helping the accusers in some way by standing up for whom they are accusing. How can this be a trap for you?

How Can We Help Ourselves Against the Accuser?

Be sober, be vigilant; because your adversary the devil walks about
like a roaring lion, seeking whom he may devour.

~ 1 Pet. 5:8-9

That no advantage may be gained over us by Satan:
for we are not ignorant of his devices.

~ 2 Cor. 2:11

The first step to overcome is we must recognize what the accuser is doing. Once we recognize the tactics of the enemy in our lives, we can move forward in how to deal with this. When dealing with the true accuser of our soul, we should only let God deal with him. I do not recommend we get into any conversations with Satan. We let God fight our battles. We don't buy into the accuser's lies. We don't listen or carry on a conversation in our mind with him either. We are God's children, and He is a great Father and will take care of it. We can take ahold of our Father's hand and put all of our trust in Him.

Praying and reading the word of God will help as the first step; and then by meeting with Him, we will receive knowledge and guidance. Letting Him take care of it is something we can put our trust in. God is with us today, and He is already in our tomorrows. We can be sure He has got this.

Keep yourselves in the love of God, looking for the mercy of our Lord Jesus Christ unto eternal life.

~ Jude 1:21

Reading and memorizing the word of God will help when accusing thoughts come to us from the accuser. Replace every negative thought with at least three positive ones. Covering the negative thought with the positive word of God and the blood of Jesus Christ will take away its power over us. Praying the word of God to increase our faith and speaking His promises out loud will build our faith. There is power in speaking the word of God into existence in our life.

The word of God is our daily bread, so we need to feast on it. Picking out some of our favorite scriptures and posting them on our bathroom mirror, so that we may read them while getting ready in the morning will help. Beginning our day claiming our promises is a great way to start our day. Reading daily word apps on our phones and tablets can be a good new habit to form. Anything we already know to help and encourage ourselves in this area, we need to do it!

Even though the accuser's plan is to keep us from God and destroy us, this does not have to be hard for us to be overcomers. I think the hard part is that it is daily. We think something is wrong with us if the fight is a daily one. So we strive to conquer this in a way, so we won't have the battle tomorrow. We get victory one day, then we put down our protection regimen the next day, celebrating our past victory because we think the accuser may be gone for a while, or we got rid of him for good. That is our first mistake. It is daily. While we are here on Earth, our fight is daily.

We should not feel surprised that the accuser rises up again right after a victory because that is who he is. The blamer. The liar. Going before God daily accusing us is his thing, but I think this is why his tactics works on us sometimes because it is daily. What better way to get our defenses worn down than to come at us every day in some way.

When our weaknesses are pointed out every day, that tactic can get us believing the accusations about us easier. We can be talked right into something, and we had nothing to do with anything—the battle has been in our minds only, the battlefield of our souls.

Remember, when we want nothing to do with sin, when we believe we are the child of the Lord, then any weakening tactic coming through our minds is the accuser. Do not claim those thoughts.

Beloved, think it not strange concerning the fiery trial which is to try you, as though some strange thing happened unto you.
~ 1 Peter 4:12

Do not be anxious about anything, but in everything by prayer and supplication with thanksgiving let your requests be made known to God. And the peace of God, which surpasses all understanding, will

guard your hearts and your minds in Christ Jesus.
Finally, brothers, whatever is true, whatever is honorable, whatever is
just, whatever is pure, whatever is lovely, whatever is commendable,
if there is any excellence, if there is anything worthy of praise,
think about these things.

~ Philippians 4:6-8

Now that we know he is a daily adversary, then daily, we should lift up the word of God; and daily, we should re-train ourselves remembering God's promises. God has made a way and has a plan of escape for each of us. Staying filled with the Holy Spirit and staying full on the word of God is our best option in recognizing the accuser and having the wisdom to deal with him.

After reading the above paragraph, we may have just heard ourselves say, "I should know this…I shouldn't have to remind myself daily, should I?" Bingo! That could be a lie we have believed from the accuser. Yes, we should remind ourselves daily of who God is, whom we are in God, and whom God is in our lives. Something this simple to a seasoned Christian may sound silly, but think on how many times throughout a normal day we can doubt. Doubt is doubting God. If we tried to keep track of this throughout one day, I think we would all be surprised as to how many times a doubting thought will actually cross our mind. Worth saying again: yes, we need to lift ourselves up daily in our most holy faith!

Wherefore comfort yourselves together, and edify one another,
even as also ye do.

~ I Thessalonians 5:11

David prayed for God's help against the false accuser in Psalm 27—*The Lord is my light and my salvation; whom shall I fear? The Lord is the strength of my life; of whom shall I be afraid? When the wicked came against me to eat up my flesh, my enemies and foes, they stumbled and fell. Though an army may encamp against me, my heart shall not fear; though war may rise against me, in this I will be confident. One thing I have desired of the Lord, that will I seek: That I may dwell in the house of the Lord all the days of my life, to behold the beauty of the Lord, and to inquire in His temple. For in the time of trouble, He shall hide me in His pavilion. In the secret place of His tabernacle, He shall hide me; He shall set me high upon a rock. And now, my head shall be lifted up above my enemies all around me; therefore I will offer sacrifices of joy in His tabernacle; I will sing, yes, I will sing praises to the Lord. Hear, O Lord, when I cry with my voice! Have mercy also upon me, and answer me. When you said, "Seek My face," My heart said to you, "Your face, Lord, I will seek." Do not hide your face from me; do not turn your servant away in anger; you have been my help; do not leave me nor forsake me, O God of my salvation. When my father and my mother forsake me, then the Lord will take care of me. Teach me your way, O Lord, and lead me in a smooth path, because of my enemies. Do not deliver me to the will of my adversaries; for false witnesses have risen against me, and such as breathe out violence. I would have lost heart, unless I had believed that I would see the goodness of the Lord in the land of the living. Wait on the Lord; be of good courage, And He shall strengthen your heart; Wait, I say, on the Lord!*

Put on the whole armor of God - *Finally, my brethren, be strong in the Lord and in the power of His might. Put on the whole armor of God that you may be able to stand against the wiles of the devil.* **Ephesians 6:10-11**

Fear not, God is our help! - *Fear not, for I am with you; be not dismayed, for I am your God; I will strengthen you; I will help you; I will uphold you with my righteous right hand.* **Isaiah, 41:10**

God is with us - *Have I not commanded you? Be strong and courageous. Do not be frightened, and do not be dismayed, for the Lord your God is with you wherever you go.* **Joshua 1:9**

He is our strength - *I can do all things through Him who strengthens me.* **Philippians 4:13**

Renew our strength, we shall walk and not faint - *He gives power to the faint, and to him who has no might, he increases strength. Even youths shall faint and be weary, and young men shall fall exhausted; but they who wait for the Lord shall renew their strength; they shall mount up with wings like eagles; they shall run and not be weary; they shall walk and not faint.* **Isaiah 40:29-31**

He will not leave us - *Be strong and courageous. Do not fear or be in dread of them, for it is the Lord your God who goes with you. He will not leave you or forsake you.* **Deuteronomy 31:6**

I shall not fear - *The Lord is my light and my salvation; whom shall I fear? The Lord is the stronghold of my life; of whom shall I be afraid?* **Psalm 27:1**

No need to fight - *You will not need to fight in this battle. Stand firm, hold your position, and see the salvation of the Lord on your behalf.* **Chronicles 20:17**

In the presence of God - *But you have upheld me because of my integrity, and set me in your presence forever.* **Psalm 41:12**

The Lord is our helper - *So we can confidently say, "The Lord is my helper; I will not fear; what can man do to me?"* **Hebrews 13:6**

Help in trouble - *God is our refuge and strength, a very present help in trouble.* **Psalm 46:1**

Guards against the evil one - *But the Lord is faithful. He will establish you and guard you against the evil one.* **II Thessalonians 3:3**

He is our rock - *My God, my rock, in whom I take refuge, my shield, and the horn of my salvation, my stronghold and my refuge, my savior; you save me from violence. I call upon the LORD, who is worthy to be praised, and I am saved from my enemies.* **II Samuel 22:3-4**

He will preserve us - *And the Lord will deliver me from every evil work and preserve me for His heavenly kingdom. To Him be glory forever and ever. Amen!* **II Timothy 4:18**

God delivers us - *Though I walk in the midst of trouble, you preserve my life; you stretch out your hand against the wrath of my enemies, and your right hand delivers me.* **Psalm 138:7**

We are safe in Him - *The name of the LORD is a strong fortress; the godly run to him and are safe.* **Proverbs 18:10**

We have peace in Him - *I have told you all this so that you may have peace in me. Here on Earth, you will have many trials and sorrows. But take heart, because I have overcome the world.* **John 16:33**

Power, love and sound mind - *For God has not given us a spirit of fear, but of power and of love and of a sound mind.* **II Timothy 1:7**

Have a good conscience - *Having a good conscience, so that, when you are slandered, those who revile your good behavior in Christ may be put to shame.* **1 Peter 3:16**

~ CHAPTER 6 REVIEW ~

- The first step to overcome is we must recognize what the accuser is doing. Once we recognize the tactics of the enemy in our lives, we can move forward in how to deal with this. What actions can you put to use to overcome?

We've Been Accused, Now What?

W e may be dealing with an accuser in one area of our lives: at work, a friend, or a family member, so now what? I would like to insert one of those "Keep Calm" signs I see everywhere; the best one for us would say:

Keep Calm

And

Walk Away

From the Accuser

We will not win a back and forth with accusers. We should not take the bait and get caught in their trap of a back and forth. Be slow to answer, slow to respond and in some cases, the next step may be not to respond at all.

When we are dealing with a person and we feel that the accusations can be turned around with the understanding of the truth; and we feel lead by the Lord to go to them in the spirit of reconciliation and deal with the situation, then please keep this scripture in mind;

Moreover if your brother sins against you, go and tell him his fault between you and him alone. If he hears you, you have gained your brother. But if he will not hear, take with you one or two more, that by

the mouth of two or three witnesses every word may be established.
And if he refuses to hear them, tell it to the church.
But if he refuses even to hear the church, let him be to you
like a heathen and a tax collector.

~ Matthew 18:15-17

If possible, we can follow this scripture in certain situations where it could apply. This scripture is not to be used to tell someone off or to get some kind of revenge for the accusations. This scripture should be used only for forgiveness and reconciliation between the people involved.

If the door is opened for us and we can put this scripture to work and it brings reconciliation, and the person listens to us and wants to make it right, then wonderful! We have won back a brother or sister.

At Work—If we are dealing with an accusing-type personality at work and we want to talk to the person about the situation, and we want to reconcile and not become an accuser ourselves here, it is best to wait until we have prayed and forgiven, so we can go with the spirit of reconciliation. If talking to the person does not help, we can seek help from the human resources department if necessary. In a lot of situations from my experience and from others that have shared with me, we may not have these first two options open to us. We just know in our heart the person would not talk with us, nor could we go to a higher up person in the company because there isn't such a position; or we know it would get us nowhere and make our job even more challenging.

It may really seem like a no-win situation. This is where prayer and our relationship with the Lord will really come into play. We will need His direction and peace. He will either work it out for us or will use it to give us something better. We could also have been placed in this situation to learn from, or our testimony may be a seed planted into the accuser's life, or someone else at work is watching both us and the accuser. We really have no idea sometimes how our life is being used for someone who is watching it.

Take note here: I don't believe we are to go through a stressful situation at work to help save someone, but I do believe God could be using us for His glory. He is not punishing us and insisting we have to stay in that kind of situation, but there could be someone He is showing our Christian behavior to. We can see here the importance that we walk with the Lord in all situations. Our giving it to Him could be the very thing that will shine into the darkness that the true accuser has planned for us.

Pray for direction and wisdom, and then move forward. A promotion could be in the works or a new job. A new job? Yes, a new job could be what will be better for us. Believe it or not: what the enemy puts in our lives to makes us miserable can be the very thing God is using to turn into something wonderful and full of blessings for us. Walk with God here; be patient and see what He is doing.

In The Family—At the sake of being redundant, we will go over each example. When dealing with an accuser, the same basics will apply in this situation also. This can be really touchy because we are *family* with this person, and family should mean something. Being close to our family has been instilled in us by God, common sense, the innate family dynamics, media and TV; and we all have the mindset of what that means.

A family member's accusations and rejection can crush us more, I believe, because of the importance of them in our lives...he or she is family. We don't want to believe this person would do something like that to us.

We may see the accuser all the time or on rare occasions; but either way, it will still be something we will have to deal with, and it will not be easy. If the accuser has spread the accusations throughout the family and many family members have been pulled into the situation, it can be overwhelming and provoke a huge response from us. We will want to react and defend ourselves immediately. The anger and hurt can take over any common sense we have. I have found that the level of hurt, shock and confusion can provoke the level of response we want to take. Taking a moment and letting our spiritual sense kick in is the best first step. Breathe and then pray.

Depending on each situation—we may have to proceed depending on the best way to handle it—but most responses should be lined up the same way we have covered. We will need to get into the place of the spirit of reconciliation. Prayer and forgiveness will help take us there. Once we have touched the Lord and He has given us personal direction, and this could take some time...so take it, we can approach the family member in hopes of a reconciliation.

It is best not to get on the phone and talk with every family member, stirring up the pot of our hurtful feelings; that will only make it worse. Talking about it will give the accusation the attention it wants. I'm not saying we can't talk about it. We don't have to be afraid to talk to someone if we are in a pure reconciliation attitude, seeking ministering help.

I do think a lot of times, we isolate ourselves as Christians because we don't want to speak ill of anything or anyone. Sometimes, we do need to talk it out with people we can trust; I am not referring to that. I am talking about when we are madder than mad, more hurt then we can imagine; we have not calmed down or prayed, and we call everyone we know. It won't help. It will make a bigger mess then we had in the beginning.

If this person will not stop in making their accusations, then we must realize what we are dealing with and go on. We can set up boundaries for this person and our relationship with him or her. Knowing the limits and not going beyond them will help with our future dealings with the accuser.

For example, if the family member is a parent, we may not feel lead to totally walk away from the relationship with the person because he or she is our parent; but we will need to set up boundaries for a more positive relationship. Since we will want to make it a somewhat livable relationship, for example, maybe we only call every other week to see how our mother or father is doing and stay on the phone a limited amount of time. Sounds silly? Sad maybe that we may have to do this, but it may have to been done for positive growth in the relationship.

We may also have to tell accusers what we will talk about and what we won't. Then we go on. We love them, but we go on. We give it to the Lord… then we go on in Him. I cannot emphasize this enough: a family member can take away from our purposed life, just

63

like anyone else. Can this happen? Yes. Is this good? No. Does it hurt, yes! But some of us may have to deal with this, and letting God lead and direct will be a wonderful help to us.

The Lord will reveal the truth in time. The Lord will fight our battle. We must glorify Him in all things. Our peace, love and forgiveness will talk to our family members more than us lowering ourselves to a back and forth battle with them in hopes of helping them. Only when they are ready to seek God for help can help come to them.

A Friend—When a good friend has accused us of something, is now spreading the accusations with others and we have just found out, we will experience shock, betrayal, hurt, embarrassment, crushed pride and shame, and the list goes on and on. The same feelings will come forth as if dealing with a co-worker or family member. We are human, and we don't like people thinking bad things about us or lying on us. Those are one hundred percent natural feelings we all share. Be comforted; we are not alone in these types of situations.

If the accusing friend appears to be open to what the truth is, and we feel he or she may have misunderstood something, we can use the guidelines of Matthew 18 here. We go in the spirit of reconciliation after we have prayed and met with the Lord.

This may feel like the same old story to some of us; or for some of us, it may be the first time we have experienced this type of person. Either way, the first or the fiftieth time, it will hurt and could hinder us to go on with purposed living. If we have experienced this in different situations with different people over time again and again, we can feel like giving up on people. We may want to isolate ourselves. We could stop wanting to attend public functions that the friend may be at. We may stop going to restaurants, hoping not to run into the accuser. Sounds great, doesn't it?

We can start living in fear. We can become nervous, looking over our shoulder at every turn. The accuser of our soul could be using this to bring us down in a final blow. If it is our first time or fiftieth time experiencing this type of attack, it doesn't matter: be assured the true accuser is still trying to do the same thing—keep us down and keep us from God.

So now, we know we've been accused. The accusations were revealed to us. So what do we do with the friend? From my experience when we rise up to defend ourselves and we call everyone who knows and we try to repair it, we take the steps to make our truth known and let everyone know we did not do what the accuser said we did, we have just now stepped right onto a minefield. This person over here tells us more hurtful things the accuser said; that person back there has sided with the accuser; and the person back there wished we hadn't involved him or her.

Now on top of all the rest of unpleasant feelings, we feel foolish, lied upon and even more troubled then we were before. Getting involved like this can also get us to act just like the accusers. We must be careful here; we can be lowered to reactions that are no better than the accusers. We can even start accusing them with things we think we know or do know about them. We can start spreading worse gossip with our friends than their accusations about us, and then who are we?

If brought to this, we will feel worse; we will feel guilty, and we will look and be just like the accuser. Then guess what? The true accuser has us better than he had us a few minutes ago and before we got involved in defending ourselves.

I have reacted in the past with no victories. My experience with reacting was hearing more hurtful things that were said by the accuser and bringing too many people into the situation, causing a larger mess. Can you believe that? Defending ourselves when the accusers are wrong about what they are accusing us of and their meaning to do us harm, and we may not see any kind of victory? Yes, that could be exactly what will happen. The accusations could grow too. With a back and forth with the friend, I do believe we are setting ourselves up to hear a lot more, and then we will have more to deal with then we had before. Once the accusers have our ear, they could be unstoppable with their accusations. The trouble becomes a BIG trouble.

Every accusation we hear about ourselves or others will influence us, and we will have to deal with them and get victory over each and every one of them to move on in our purposed life.

I did not see anything good come out of my situation by defending myself. I only heard more than I should have and was put into bigger mind-blowing accusations that I had to work through. The only victories I have had are when I've given the entire situation to the Lord. And that's the truth.

There may be situations where we must stand up and say it is a falsehood and that we are not guilty of what's accused. For instance, if at the job we are accused of stealing something and we did not steal anything, we must say the truth to whom this may concern. In a legal case or something of that kind of nature, please use common sense here.

In circumstances that are different then the above, I have to recommend again not defending ourselves, but let God. I also recommend doing a lot of soul searching in these situations. The reason is to come humbly before the Lord and let Him speak to us and seek the wisdom we will need. Wisdom for what is truly going on, wisdom for how to deal and wisdom for how we should pick and choose our future friendships. This last statement is not to say we could have done anything better or to say we had done something wrong with picking this friend who has become an accuser. People are people; we all fall short, and we will all at one time or another run into this type of situation. Seeking friendship wisdom is being a better person ourselves. The more we grow, the wiser we are in our relationships.

Also, searching our own heart here is very important; and taking a look in the mirror will help us stay on the right track. We are not to fear friendships; we are not to isolate ourselves after experiencing this kind of hurt; but knowing more, growing more and learning more of God's wisdom is a great tool in our daily lives. Any wisdom He can impart to us in dealing with people—we should be lining up for the class. There truly is not a recipe to avoid these people forever; a part of this is life, and a huge part is if the true accuser knows he can hurt us by using people we have become friends with, then he will try to find someone who will fill the job.

We may think one of the following;

1. But aren't we letting someone get away with it if we don't confront him or her?
2. Shouldn't we stop accusers; they could do this to someone else?
3. I know this person will listen to me; I will fix this.
4. Accusers need to be stopped, and I'm the one to do it.

All of those are normal thoughts. Accusers do need to stop, and people do need to know the truth; but going after someone like this will not correct much, if anything. Again, unless this person wants to change with God's help, there is nothing we can do that will change the pattern.

The accusers could love the chaos they are stirring up; and if they do, that will feed the accusing more. Sometimes by reacting, we can even look like the bad guy, which is exactly their plan. Since the accusers have worked hard to not make themselves known, by reacting, it could look like we are the accuser. If we start going around saying what they did, it wouldn't take much for us to look just like them. Most people will not know what we are talking about. Some will know and understand, but those are the people we never had to defend ourselves to anyway because they have recognized the accusers.

At Church—If these types of situations are going on in a church setting, the same steps as our other relationships will also apply here. If our accuser is a person who we attend church with, confusion will be at the top of our hurts and emotions. We don't expect that kind of behavior from fellow God forgiven Christians do we? But what better way for the true accuser to get at some of us who have found a refuge in the church. He would love to stop us before we even get started. One of his tactics can be sending accusations through someone in our church who shares our Christian faith.

Are we seeing a pattern to how he works? We may not want to attend church. We may feel so overwhelmed by the hurt the accusation caused, we can't see ourselves entering the doors again. Then our thoughts will go in every direction to really cement in what the true accuser wants us to believe. *Weren't we supposed to find forgiveness in the church? Weren't we supposed to find love, peace and joy? Oh, no, who knows what they are saying?* We may feel more lost then before we were found by Jesus.

I have seen new Christians especially attacked in this type of area. Christians who think they are the seasoned old saints of God can point fingers and accuse new Christians of things that they really know nothing about. I want to remind us here, we are not aware of all that God is doing in someone's life, nor is it our business. Stepping into the accuser's seat here can be dangerous to our own walk with the Lord and to the soul God is working on. I have seen some people in the church use their influence and elevate their fault finding to great heights, and they call it ministry. We need to be very careful we are not acting as the accuser. Again, let God. We are not God, and He's got it handled.

Depending on the situation, the leadership of the church could help with the steps of dealing with this. Counselors in the church may be able to help in these situations also. Again, the approach here should be to reconcile all parties concerned.

We may be thinking on how unfair it is. We may still want to see the truth revealed. Their accusations have made us feel rejected. Rejection will cause anger. Anger causes bitterness. We truly do not want any part of these problems settling into our spirit. And that is why it is so important for us to walk in the wisdom of what we are truly dealing with. The best way to settle this is to keep giving it to God, for He fights our battles, and the battle is the Lord's.

A hint here to the ending of the story…God will show up and give light to the truth in His timing. The falsehoods and accusations will show their fruit eventually. If we stand with God, the truth will stand in our lives.

It takes courage to stand up to an accuser, but it takes even more courage for us not to defend ourselves and let God do it. Pray and wait. Pray and let God. Pray and be restored in the Lord. In a moment, in the twinkling of an eye, the Lord can heal and restore everything in us that was taken away by the accuser's accusations.

~ CHAPTER 7 REVIEW ~

- We will not win a back and forth with accusers, but what stood out to you that you can do?

- We may think how unfair it is when dealing with an accusing type person. How can giving it to God, for He fights our battles, be beneficial to you?

The Separating

In the title of this book, I use the word *separate*. To separate means to withdraw, keep apart, disunite, part-company, disperse, space apart and to become divided from. Believe it or not—to separate ourselves from the accuser may be the hardest part for some of us to do.

Our natural positive personality traits are dependable, fair, discreet, impartial, optimistic, encouraging, capable, independent, dutiful, reliable, trusting, helpful and humble to name a few. Taking a look at those positive traits in us shows us in part the reason we have a hard time separating ourselves from the accuser.

Making decisions to withdraw, part company or put a lot of space between us and the accuser is not what most of us like to do; it doesn't have a good sound to it. Part company? Walk away? Give up? We want to be a good person. We want to be fair. We want to help people. We want to be encouraging. We want to fix things. We want what we want. And we want it to work.

We don't want to walk away, fail or give up on anything or anyone; and the word separate can cause such a final feeling in all of us. Even if we are separating ourselves from something really bad, it still gives some of us the feeling that we gave up. It has a negative sound to it because of how we feel about the word. The feeling towards the word can cause us to doubt if we should separate ourselves from an accusing relationship. And doubt will cause us not to act, even when we should.

Most of us, I do believe, feel we would separate ourselves from Satan, the true accuser of the brethren—goodness who wouldn't, right? We would be surprised to see how many of us haven't separated ourselves from the true accuser. For many reasons, one being we didn't even know he existed so much in our daily life until we've read some of this book, or we've never drawn a line in the sand and taken a stand against his lies. We can also play with the thoughts we get in our mind from him. We can even entertain them long enough that we draw ourselves closer to what the true accuser is saying to us. Can we carry on a conversation with the enemy of our soul? Really? If we are listening to him, then yes, we are talking to him. A one-sided conversation would still be classified as a conversation.

To separate from the true accuser is to not go there. Withdraw from every thought he sends. Part company with the temptations he teases us with. We need to run, disperse and go in the opposite direction. We need to be totally divided from him and far away from the line that separates us from him.

Be not deceived, the enemy is out there. Training ourselves up in our most holy faith will help in the separation process. It is in the knowing, knowing the accuser roars like a lion seeking to defeat us. Resist that devil. When we become so full of Jesus, there will be no room for the true accuser to interject his thoughts in us. And if and when he tries, because he never gives up, we will not be as affected as when we were not aware.

That the God of our Lord Jesus Christ, the Father of glory, may give unto you the spirit of wisdom and revelation in the knowledge of him.

~ Ephesians 1:17

Lest Satan should take advantage of us; for we are not ignorant of his devices.

~ II Cor. 2:11

So the great dragon was cast out, that serpent of old, called the Devil and Satan, who deceives the whole world; he was cast to the earth, and his angels were cast out with him.

~ Rev. 12:9

The devil, who deceived them, was cast into the lake of fire and brimstone where[a] the beast and the false prophet are. And they will be tormented day and night forever and ever.

~ Rev. 20:10

Nor give place to the devil.

~ Ephesians 4:27

Let's cover now the situations where some of the accusations in our lives are coming from an accusing-type person. I would like to remind us here that being an accusing-type person does not mean being processed by the devil. We also need to be reminded that we are not fighting people, but it is spiritual warfare.

Separating ourselves from this person may or may not be easy. If this is a friend or family member, it can be very difficult. To withdraw with new boundaries or disunite from a relationship will not be an easy task. I would like to point out here that in some cases we may need to totally separate ourselves until God reopens the door; but in most cases, separating here means new boundaries: we are not an ear any longer, and we are not listening to this kind of behavior any longer. We are drawing a line in the sand. We are setting up new limits with these people; and if they want a relationship with us, they will have to stay in the guidelines of those limits.

Some of us may be so ready to separate in some situations because we are worn out from the hurt, or we are just plain sick of all it. But it may be the accusers who are not ready to separate or follow our new guidelines for our relationship with them.

Earlier, we read how the situation could get worse by trying to separate ourselves. This could be true, if we change up our relationship with accusing people, then that will signal to them that something is up. Once they think they have been found out, something they never want to happen, they will have to try to accuse us more to make themselves look better. This is when they will usually really act up. I have found this is when we know we weren't going crazy by what we were feeling. Their accusing fruits could really show now. They will want to hide behind their accusations. We may even see some desperate measures here; by that I mean, if they have accused badly before, their accusations could really reach new levels now.

If we were the accuser's ear and we have realized what we are dealing with and we are trying to pull away and find some new safer boundaries in this relationship, we will be the enemy; and typically, we could find here that the accuser will start accusing us.

If we were the accused, the accusations could get worse. The accusers seem to be very astute in these types of situations; they do seem to have some kind of discernment. Again, this is not to scare us but prepare us. I do believe in these types of situations we are still called to separate.

Separating is letting God. If any good can come out of the situation, the best hands to put this in are God's. Knowing that can give us extreme peace. Trusting God to handle our battles will be the best for all concerned. We have no idea what God is doing in this person's life—that can also help us stay on track—that we don't try to fix the accusing situation. God will work all things for the good, for both us and the accuser.

And we know that all things work together for good to those who love
God, to those who are the called according to His purpose.
~ Romans 8:28

One of the first steps of action, when we realize we have been dealing with an accusing-type person, is forgiveness. Forgiving can be made easier if we realize we are not fighting against flesh and blood. All accusations start with the true accuser of our souls. We should not fall into any kind of judgment here either, no matter how hurt we are. Guarding our thoughts here is using wisdom.

Give it to the Lord. Just hand it over. We may not feel forgiveness in the beginning because of the level of accusations and our raw feelings. I do believe we can hand that over to God, too. He can help us forgive. We can forgive in the most impossible situations with His help. We may think not, but with Him all things are possible. Forgiving them will be so freeing for us in every aspect of our life.

I have found that when I've handed the whole situation over to the Lord—I don't know when, nor do I know how He did it—but it was gone. I felt one hundred percent compassion towards the person who accused me falsely. I was not hurt or mad at what they did any longer. And by some miracle, I saw them through His eyes. I was free from what the enemy tried to do through them. The bad was turned to good, and that is our promise from the Lord. Praise God!

The people who fall into this accusing category really need our prayers. They cannot be walking in the peace of God always accusing and blaming others. Somewhere along the way, they have believed the lies of the enemy and have been deceived themselves. Forgiving them and separating ourselves from their tactics, and no longer giving them an ear or response, could be the one thing that will talk to them and help them. God could very well use our testimony of peace and forgiveness towards them. If they do not want help—that is entirely up to them—but by forgiving them, we will be good with God and our purposed life, glorify Him with our testimony.

If we continue listening to the person who accuses, either about us or someone else, I do believe that will vex our soul. By separating, we will stop hearing. Lot was vexed in his soul by hearing bad conversations. Hearing accusations, falsehoods and gossip is not a good conversation. We have been commanded to think on good things, whatsoever is pure and of a good report.

Vex—To bring trouble, to irritate, distress, to worry, to cause perplexity, annoy, to puzzle, to bring physical distress, to debate at length.

And delivered just Lot, vexed with the filthy conversation of the
wicked: For that righteous man dwelling among them,
in seeing and hearing, vexed his righteous soul
from day to day with their unlawful deeds.

~ II Peter 2:7

Finally, brethren, whatsoever things are true, whatsoever things are
honest, whatsoever things are just, whatsoever things are pure,
whatsoever things are lovely, whatsoever things are of good report; if
there be any virtue, and if there be any praise, think on these things.

~ Philippians 4:8

But let none of you suffer as a murderer, or as a thief, or as an
evildoer, or as a busybody in other men's matters.

~ I Peter 4:15

Be not deceived: evil communications corrupt good manners.

~ I Corinthians 15:33

Do not be unequally yoked together with unbelievers. For what
fellowship has righteousness with lawlessness? And what communion
has light with darkness?

~ II Corinthians 6:14

No one engaged in warfare entangles himself with the affairs of this life, that he may please him who enlisted him as a soldier.

~ II Tim. 2:4

I am the vine, ye are the branches: He that abideth in me, and I in him, the same bringeth forth much fruit: for without me, ye can do nothing.

~ John 15:5

So, here we are, we know we have heard from God—we are to have no part of an accusing-type relationship. It is not good for us or the person who is accusing. Receiving this knowledge, we are now going to take the necessary steps to separate ourselves from this kind of behavior. We have just read from the chapters of this book, and we feel motivated. But some of us are still thinking: *What should I do in my situation? Oh no, I'm nearing the end of the book, and I still haven't quite got it.* Even after a good church service or we've read another good self-help book or in prayer, when God himself gave us direction on what to do, we can still feel unsure on how to go about obeying and taking that first step in what we need to do.

I believe the first step is knowing;

- Know whom God is to us

- Know the Word of God

- Know whom we are in Him

- Know His Voice

- Know our sins are forgiven

- Know God leads us

- Know God knows

- Know God guides us to all truth

- Know God

Once we truly claim who we are and are filled up in the knowledge of the Lord Jesus Christ, and we are walking with Him…feeling confident in whom we are in Jesus, we will trust in His strength to get us through. Believe this, the accuser will flee! And if there are a few tag-a-long accusers along our way, and there very well may be, we will know how to deal with their accusations, falsehoods and lies.

~ CHAPTER 8 REVIEW ~

- The word, separate, was used in the title of this book. How can separating yourself from the accuser in your life benefit you?

- Separating is letting God. What steps could you see yourself doing towards separating and why?

CHAPTER 9

What if I'm an Accuser?

After learning the traits of an accuser in the first chapters and seeing that we may be an accuser, what do we do then? If we have seen our personality traits and our behavior along the line of the accuser—we have blamed people in our life for all the bad things that have happened to us; we are a fault finder; we have a critical spirit or spread falsehoods for our gain—then this is knowledge to us, and knowledge is good. The first step to good Christian growth is knowledge.

We are wrong if we act this way; these are not the characteristics of a mature Christian, and we need to change our behavior immediately. If we are a new babe in Christ and we've never given our accusing behavior a thought, now is the time.

Accusing behavior is a deception of the enemy, and there are many reasons why we could have fallen into that rut. Here are just a few examples of what could have started us on the accusing path: some of us have been trained to do this by other accusers; it is all we have seen and heard our whole lives; we have been hurt somewhere in our past and blame seems to be the only comfort road we want to take; or we fight against such great insecurities and have believed the lies from the true accuser of the brethren, and we feel we have to tear others down to build ourselves back up.

Jealousy seems to be a big motivator in falling into the accusing rut. Comparing one's life with another can prompt this kind of behavior. Self-hate and condemnation is another one, and they could have us bound in such a way we are not even recognizing what we do until the accusations are out of our mouths. And then we are so empty on the inside, we don't have the strength to pull them back in until it is too late.

One of the most common ruts to fall into is to accuse when we have been accused. This is the back and forth that was described in an earlier chapter. They accuse; we accuse; they accuse, and then we accuse in what we think is our defense. We are not defending ourselves with accusations going back and forth. We are being drawn in, and now we are used in the exact same fashion as the person who was accusing us.

We can generalize the entire human race at times because of how we've been treated by some. This example is the one I see the most and where we should continually work at stopping any accusing thoughts that can pop up. We can accuse people immediately in our minds, just because of the way we have been treated in the past.

For instance, we can think all people, in all churches, are rude because someone was rude to us when we visited a church years ago; or we can think all new friends will eventually hurt us because we have been hurt by people we thought were friends in the past. Or it can be something as simple as we have received poor help by most waitresses in the past, so we peg all waitresses to be of the same quality. We can be in the accusing rut: *Well, that is how we've been treated in the certain situations in the past.* So across the board, we think they are all guilty.

We need to see how wrong this kind of thinking is. For one reason, we are acting as the accuser; and for another, we will miss every good thing coming our way because we have generalized everything and everyone into the same box and have believed a lie.

Some of us have never looked in the mirror, ever. We have never double-checked our motives in talking about people or anything else we do. That could be a huge lack of knowledge on our part, or there is no desire to do what is right anymore because we feel so dead inside.

Any of these reasons by no means makes an excuse for our accusing behavior. The reasons, whatever they are, have been a door for us to be used by the enemy of our soul. Let us not be deceived any longer. If we walk in these accusing traits, we need to stop them. They are a work of the flesh. They are a huge negative in our life. We will not get ahead being an accuser. We will not have peace walking and talking in falsehoods. We do not have to accuse others to better ourselves. We will not be seen in a better light by blaming others. We will only get better by looking in the mirror and seeing the truth. Facing the truth and walking in the truth will take us to where God has planned for us.

Some of us could be thinking right now and justifying our accusing behavior, "But I only repeat what the truth is, or that person really deserved what I said, or someone needed to know about what they did, right?" Speaking of things that do not concern us is none of our business. Nor is gossip of any kind good. How do we know what really is the truth when we are repeating something we've heard? When repeating tales, what are our motives? Jesus is the only person who knows the truth in a matter, and He has asked us to keep a bridle on our tongue.

Thou shalt not go up and down as a talebearer among thy people; neither shalt thou stand against the blood of thy neighbor: I am the Lord.
~ Leviticus 19:16

Let no corrupt word proceed out of your mouth, but what is good for necessary edification, that it may impart grace to the hearers.
~ Ephesians 4:29

A perverse man sows strife, and a whisperer separates the best of friends.
~Proverbs 16:28

If anyone among you thinks he is religious, and does not bridle his tongue but deceives his own heart, this one's religion is useless.
~ James 1:26

Keep your tongue from evil, and your lips from speaking deceit.
~ Psalm 34:13

And besides they learn to be idle, wandering about from house to house, and not only idle but also gossips and busybodies, saying things which they ought not.
~ I Timothy 5:13

Jesus loves us and is faithful to forgive us for our sins. None of us are without sin, and all of us need Jesus in every area of our life. We are truly in need of Him in all things. All we have to do is run into the open arms of Jesus and receive His love and forgiveness. If we have found ourselves here among accuser-type behavior, then it stops here. We don't beat ourselves up, and we do not let the true accuser attack our mind as we are on a new road of behavior. We go to Jesus... believe me, the Lord has got this. He is our help in time of trouble!

After we have asked for forgiveness, there may be people we have accused, blamed, criticized or said falsehoods about, that we may need to go to and reconcile, especially if they knew of our accusations and have been hurt by them. Acknowledging what we did and being able to make things right is so freeing for our soul. It may seem like an awful place to be in, but it is not. Not being bound by the enemy and his lies is a wonderful way to live. Being set free in our forgiveness that is offered from our Lord and Savior will remove the oppression and the chains from this kind of behavior.

If we confess our sins, He is faithful and just to forgive us our sins, and to cleanse us from all unrighteousness.
~ I John 1:9

Then Peter said unto them, Repent, and be baptized every one of you in the name of Jesus Christ for the remission of sins, and ye shall receive the gift of the Holy Ghost.
~ Acts 2:38

For all have sinned, and come short of the glory of God.
~ Romans 3:23

For whosoever shall call upon the name of the Lord shall be saved.

~ Romans 10:13

If we say that we have no sin, we deceive ourselves,
and the truth is not in us.

~ I John 1:8

For by grace are ye saved through faith; and that not of yourselves:
it is the gift of God.

~ Ephesians 2:8

And forgive us our debts, as we forgive our debtors.

~ Matthew 6:12

Let none of you imagine evil in your hearts against his neighbor, and
love no false oath. For all these are things that I hate, saith the Lord.

~ Zechariah 8:17

If you really fulfill the royal law according to the Scripture, "You shall
love your neighbor as yourself," and you do well.

~ James 2:8

For all the law is fulfilled in one word, even in this:
You shall love your neighbor as yourself.

~ Galatians 5:14

- Accusing behavior is a deception of the enemy, and there are many reasons why we could have fallen into that rut. What examples stood out to you?

- Looking in the mirror can be so beneficial in helping us stay on track in our spiritual life. In what ways does this talk to you?

Concluding Thoughts

The purpose of this book is to get us to think; it does not have all the answers. But by seeking knowledge, our God will give us the answers we need in all things. The message in this book is to bring knowledge to us about the tactics of the true accuser. We are not fighting people, though it may seem like that at times. It is truly a spiritual warfare.

How about those days when we knew something was wrong? We couldn't quite grab ahold of what we were fighting, but we were distressed anyway. We felt affected; something was off; our thoughts were in strange places or torn between two things. We felt pulled, negative or defensive? Taking a good look at whom we are hanging out with during our day can be very beneficial. And by that, I mean people or the thoughts in our mind. We don't need to keep an ongoing conversation with bad thoughts or keep company with people who are accusing and stunting our spiritual growth. It is not a sign of weakness, but a sign of strength to let go and let God.

It is so important that God is first in our daily life. I do believe there is an easy way to do this. We need to mentally take the Lord Jesus Christ everywhere we go. We must make the conscious effort of believing He is with us every day and all day. He is with us—so why not walk in that truth? No doubting and no second-guessing. Just a firm belief that He is.

When we wake up in the morning, we should train our thoughts every day to go to the Lord first. What is His plan for our day? His will for our day? And more important for most of us, what are His promises for our day? Knowing who He is and who we are in Him is very important. Who do we say He is and who do we say we are? Know the answers to those questions! These are steps of faith, and we should walk in them.

We should ignore any feelings of unbelief; be as a child and even pretend if we have to. By walking in faith and doing this, even if it wasn't a part of us before, it will be a part of us soon. Even if in the first few steps we feel we are pretending, not feeling it, we will not be pretending for long. Believing will bring faith, and God will bless our sincere heart.

With God first in our lives, we will be led by Him, not wandering around in our day lost with random thoughts triggering off in our minds, which we don't recognize, and those thoughts having no real purpose.

Without a dream, a purpose, a vision or a hope, we can be an open door to the accuser of our soul. Staying focused in our thoughts and reigning in any unexplained or doubting thoughts will help us walk in the power that God has given us. Don't give up, and don't be surprised if we are reigning in random thoughts that bring us down every few seconds, minutes or hours, just keep doing it. By letting this be part of our daily walk, we will walk in God's love for ourselves and for others.

We will never be without trouble, but we don't have to stumble around in trouble either.

Yet man is born to trouble, as the sparks fly upward.
~ Job 5:7

The true accuser is daily looking for an open door to attack us or use us. But these are God's promises to us: God will take care of us. He will compensate us if we fall short. He will correct anything we may have gotten ourselves into. God doesn't make mistakes, and we know He made us, proving we are not a mistake.

I want us to know that God loves each and every one of us more than we can imagine. I don't think we could ever say that enough to people, nor do I believe we hear it enough. He is a giving Father, a forgiving God. He is our protector and more than capable of delivering us from the accuser's hand. We need to just talk to Him; we don't have to have long, fancy prayers—we just need to speak to Him. Having an ongoing conversation with Him all day is a great plan for our relationship with Him. Talk to God about the little things too? Yes, we should talk to Him about everything! Then wait and listen for Him to talk back with us.

The Lord recently gave me a word that is so powerful, and I would like to pass it on to you. I am passing this on with great faith, that it will do for you what it did for me:

The LORD is thy keeper:
the LORD is thy shade upon thy right hand.
~ Psalm 121:5

I just love what He showed me in this; and I do believe if we will grab ahold of this word, it is a life changer for us. The Lord is standing beside us all day long. He is the shade on our right side. How powerful if we truly walked this way, believing our right side was shadowed all day by the Lord. How powerful if we believed this every day, that He was there and taking care of us all day long and not let one negative thought take that away. How powerful!

It is not about us; it is all about Him. If we put Him first in all things and let Him be the shadow on our right side, we will be totally protected from all the accusations of the accuser. Will they still come? Yes, but now, we know what we know; and watch out, accuser, because we are the knowledgeable child of the King. The accuser's devices and tactics will fall away from us like the weak and broken arrows that they are. They will not touch us, nor hurt us.

We have a destiny in God, and that destiny is as important to God, as it should be to us. What a waste if we were to squander it. Who we are and what we are in God is so valuable. We have every opportunity before us. We truly do. I wish these words would wrap around each of us, bringing belief with them, so none of us reading this would ever doubt again.

I truly hate seeing the true accuser get a foothold in someone's mind. I hate seeing people deceived, lied to, believing a falsehood, doubting everything good in their lives or full of guilt.

I hate to see relationships crumbling because someone has believed the accuser. I hate the destruction left from the accuser's path. Let's do our part by stopping it. We can make a difference in our lives and in the lives of others.

I would like to remind us that when the accusations come and they are truth, part truth or a lie, no matter what they are, it is all about the accuser, not us. It is the accuser's problem not ours. The accusers want to mix that up though; they want their problem to be our problem. That is the change up the accuser wants in our daily focus. However the accuser comes, they will want the focus on us, not them.

Having patience here will help. Patience is enduring under bad circumstances and the willingness of forgiving without getting back. Resisting the devil and not feeling sorry for ourselves will help also. Giving the whole situation to God and not making ourselves the focus will make all the difference in the world to us. Remember, it is not what we did or about us.

If we are worrying and concerned about the separating part, we need not be anxious; we need to do what we know to do and get out of God's way. If we are still questioning what does God want us to do, then the very next step is what has He told us to do?

If we only have one little piece of direction, then that is what we should do. The next step will follow. Just do what we know to do. This is a great principal to live by, not just on this subject but in all subjects. We need to ask ourselves when we are still questioning and seeking an answer in something: Do we know one thing we can do that we know was from God? Then that is the next step we take, and we just keep taking that step until we get the next step of direction from God.

We need to let God. We cannot fix people. We cannot change people. But what we can do is pray, love ourselves, love others and not let the accuser accuse anymore. We can be a closed ear to the accuser and just let God!

Let us *not* have more faith in doubt, fear and shame then we do in God. His gift of the Holy Spirit is a gift for all of us. We can live in a supernatural, powerful way. We can know what we should avoid. We can know who we should avoid. We can live in an abundance of His power every day.

One last thought: I would like to take us to a place in our minds where three powerful words were spoken, "*It is finished.*" Those words were spoken at a very special place, and that place is Calvary. Jesus made a victory cry before He commended His spirit to the Father, and that was, "It is finished!" Everything we could ever imagine was done for us and more. It was all taken care of right then and there. It was done for us. It was finished.

It was a victory cry. Our God was victorious on the cross. Jesus was victorious for us! So how could we in good conscience neglect the gift that was given to us and the gifts that are within us? Let's make up our mind right now. We can do this. We can become the positive in a world of negative. We can overcome the accusations. We can get out of the way. We can forgive and let God fight our battles. We can overcome anything sent our way with the Lord Jesus Christ.

The truth doesn't set us free if we don't know it… know the truth, and the truth will set us free.

Then you will know the truth,
and the truth will set you free.
~ John 8:32

~ CHAPTER 10 REVIEW ~

- The purpose of this book is to get us to think. What good thoughts have you decided to put into action?

- You can see that we need to let God. You cannot fix people or all situations, nor can you change them. But what can you do?

References:

King James Version and New King James Version

www.biblegateway.com

www.qoogle.com

www.freedictionary.com

www.dictionary.com

www.meriam-webster.com

.